...and best-known travel brands,
Thomas Cook are the experts in travel.

...rs our
...ecrets
...world,
...th of
...ravel.

...your
...travelling companion on your next trip
and benefit from our unique heritage.

Thomas Cook **pocket** guides

BIRMINGHAM

Thomas
Cook

...nce 1873

Written by Gordon Lethbridge

Published by Thomas Cook Publi
A division of Thomas Cook Tour Operations Limited
Company Registration no. 3772199 England
The Thomas Cook Business Park, Unit 9, Coningsby Road,
Peterborough PE3 8SB, United Kingdom
Email: books@thomascook.com, Tel: + 44 (0) 1733 416477
www.thomascookpublishing.com

Produced by Cambridge Publishing Management Limited
Burr Elm Court, Main Street, Caldecote CB23 7NU
www.cambridgepm.co.uk

ISBN: 978-1-84848-458-0

First edition © 2010 Thomas Cook Publishing
Text © Thomas Cook Publishing
Cartography supplied by Redmoor Design, Tavistock, Devon
Map data © OpenStreetMap contributors CC-BY-SA, www.openstreetmap.org,
www.creativecommons.org

Series Editor: Karen Beaulah
Production/DTP: Steven Collins

Printed and bound in Spain by GraphyCems

Cover photography © Thomas Cook Publishing

CONTENTS

SYMBOLS KEY

The following symbols are used throughout this book:

ⓐ address ⊕ telephone ⓕ fax ⓦ website address ⓔ email
ⓛ opening times ⓝ public transport connections ⓘ important

The following symbols are used on the maps:

𝒊	information office	○	city
🛍	shopping	○	large town
✉	post office	○	small town
✈	airport	=	motorway
✚	hospital	—	main road
🛡	police station	—	minor road
🚌	bus station	—	railway
🚆	railway station		
▮	POI (point of interest)		
✝	cathedral		
❶	numbers denote featured cafés, restaurants & venues		

PRICE CATEGORIES

The ratings below indicate average price rates for a double
room per night, including breakfast:
£ under £40 ££ £40–80 £££ over £80
The typical cost for a three-course meal without drinks
is as follows:
£ under £20 ££ £20–35 £££ over £35

❿ *Canals lie at the heart of this vibrant city*

INTRODUCING
Birmingham

Introduction

Even those who pass through on the train or speed round Birmingham's motorways can see that Birmingham has thrown off its old image as a city of grime and dirt. Although it is still a manufacturing base, in recent years it has reinvented itself as a centre for business, conferences and retail, as well as key sporting and cultural events. With a young population swelled by students of its three universities and numerous colleges, the city has a youthful, edgy buzz to it.

Birmingham is a city that has provided the impetus and motivation for many inventors and discoveries over the years. Gas street lighting, for example, was invented here. The city also gained renown for manufacturing armaments, from the English Civil War onwards, and it was from the factories of Birmingham that the World War II Spitfire fighter plane was produced. Today, the city provides innovation in the fields of technology, the visual arts and architecture.

Writers such as J R R Tolkien and Washington Irving were inspired by their time in Birmingham, while major British institutions such as Bird's Custard, HP Sauce, Typhoo Tea, Cadbury and the Mini (the car, not the skirt) originated from here.

After the 1970s, as industry went into decline, far-sighted city fathers made the decision to reinvent Birmingham as a business and convention centre and to lure many of the arts to Birmingham. In 1980 the great English conductor Simon Rattle took on the City of Birmingham Symphony Orchestra and made it one of the world's greats; new theatres were built which gave upcoming talent a chance; and arts venues were improved, enticing artistic companies to make their home in the city, most notably the Sadler's Wells Royal Ballet Company (now the Birmingham Royal Ballet). The city is awash with sculptures and monuments both classic and contemporary, visible proof that art and architecture play an important role in local public spending.

At the time of writing, Birmingham was on the shortlist for Capital of Culture 2013 – a far cry from the clanging and clanking of its industrial furnaces and smoky factories for which the city was renowned in the 19th and early 20th centuries.

◖ *The canals were crucial to Birmingham's commercial success*

When to go

SEASONS & CLIMATE

Like most of Britain, Birmingham has a temperate climate that can be fickle at times. Generally speaking, however, July and August have the highest average temperatures and January and February the lowest.

The wonderful displays of flowers and blossom in spring and the vibrant colours of autumn make these two seasons a good time to visit the city's parks and gardens. The balmy air of late spring and early autumn and the sunny days of summer are the best time to cycle or walk the canal paths that radiate from the centre of Birmingham out through its suburbs.

Given the cultural nature of the city there is always something going on at any time of the year. However, May to September are the best months for festivals, open-air concerts and fairs. In the six weeks leading up to Christmas, Birmingham's shopping centres can become crowded, but it is still worth visiting for the large German Christmas Market, where traders are attracted from Birmingham's twin city, Frankfurt.

FESTIVALS
February
Chinese New Year celebrations with fire crackers, lanterns and parades in the Chinese Quarter.

March
The **St Patrick's Day** celebrations are Europe's largest outside Dublin.

July
The **Birmingham International Jazz Festival** is one of Europe's leading jazz festivals. It takes place at 70 venues across the city over two weeks in July and attracts international stars.

September
ArtsFest is the largest free arts festival in Europe and takes place over three days. Dates vary.

October
The **Comedy Festival** draws attention to the city's vibrant comedy scene. Both local and national comedians give you something to laugh about. October is also the month of the **Birmingham Book Festival**, with its diverse programme of discussions, lectures and workshops from a varied menu of writers, poets, novelists, journalists and storytellers.

⬤ *Spring flowers in Cannon Hill Park*

History

According to the Domesday Book, in 1086 Birmingham was just a small hamlet of nine households worth only 20 shillings. In 1166 Peter de Birmingham, lord of the manor, was granted a royal charter to hold a market, thus transforming what had now become a small village into a market town. Soon the town became a centre of commerce for the surrounding agricultural area, and smiths and craftsmen established themselves here.

Farm implements were forged in the town and when the English Civil War began in the mid-17th century, it was found that weapons such as pikes and swords could be easily

◔ *Lord Nelson stands guard over the Bullring*

produced in large quantities for the Parliamentary troops. This established Birmingham's reputation as a manufacturing centre for small armaments, which continued until after World War II.

During the Industrial Revolution, the town prospered and became a centre for industry, particularly engineering and metalworking. Skills learned were also used for working with precious metals. Jewellery craftsmen began setting up workshops in what is now the Jewellery Quarter. Birmingham became a centre for innovation, which it has remained to this day – 50 per cent of all UK patents still come from Birmingham.

Due to its position in the centre of England, Birmingham soon became a transport hub, with canals, railways and finally roads converging there. By the early 19th century, Birmingham was the second-largest population centre in Britain, and in 1889 was granted city status by Queen Victoria herself.

Being an industrial area and producer of armaments meant that Birmingham was a prime target for the Luftwaffe during World War II. It suffered heavily in the Blitz and rebuilding and redevelopment in the 1950s and 60s was rapid and ill-conceived. As industry moved overseas to cheaper labour markets, Birmingham's importance as a manufacturing centre declined.

But the city of Birmingham has reacted to this downturn by reinventing itself. Much of the concrete of the 1960s has gone, replaced by architecture that is breathtaking in its audacity. New squares have been formed and old ones transformed. Historic buildings have been restored and the canals cleared and opened up. World-class venues have been built.

Birmingham is looking forward into the 21st century with pride and confidence.

Culture

Birmingham has a thriving arts and music scene, which has helped make it on to the shortlist for European Capital of Culture 2013. There are several world-class venues for music, as well as edgy, contemporary art galleries that happily sit alongside the Victorian and Edwardian edifices containing more classical works of art. The City of Birmingham Symphony Orchestra (CBSO) has become internationally renowned, as has the Birmingham Royal Ballet. Symphony Hall is home to the CBSO, and the Hippodrome Theatre is where ballet-lovers and aficionados head.

The city gave birth to repertory theatre and both the Birmingham Repertory Theatre (commonly called 'The Rep') and The Old Rep still put on productions, many of which are experimental and innovative.

The Birmingham Jazz Festival, held in the first two weeks of July, has an established reputation that attracts performers from all over the world. ArtsFest in September presents free arts and cultural events all over the city.

With venues like the National Exhibition Centre (NEC), the National Indoor Arena (NIA), the Town Hall and Symphony Hall, Birmingham is an ideal location for major concert tours, from hard rock groups to classical orchestras.

Following in the footsteps of great 'Brummie' comedians like Jasper Carrott and Tony Hancock, Birmingham's comedy scene attracts both national and local stand-up comics.

◗ *The magnificent classical façade of the Town Hall*

 MAKING THE MOST OF
Birmingham

Shopping

Ever since Peter de Birmingham was granted a charter to hold a market, the centre of the city has been a 'shopping centre'. The market of 1166 was the predecessor of today's mega shopping malls and markets of the Bullring. Modern shopping centres sit cheek by jowl with the original Victorian arcades.

The Bullring's cutting-edge structure is the second incarnation of the retail centre; the original mall was built in the 1960s and though iconic in its day – it was the largest covered shopping centre outside the United States – by the 1980s had become old and tired and was eventually demolished. The redeveloped Bullring (now spelled Bullring to set it apart from the old Bull Ring) was reopened in 2003 and its 160 shops now attract over 20 million shoppers annually. It has a **Selfridges**, housed in an iconic building, and the second-largest Debenhams store in the country. Along with the indoor shopping centre, traditional streets, open markets and squares have been restored to the site.

Next door to the Bullring shopping centre is the Pavilions, its four floors of shops home to better-known brands. A short walk away is **The Mailbox**, the former Royal Mail sorting office that now houses chic boutiques, high-end retailers such as Harvey Nichols, Armani and Jaeger, and trendy café-bars.

Two Victorian arcades – the **Great Western Arcade** and the **Burlington Arcade** – have been restored and contain small boutique retailers that cater to the more independent shopper. If you prefer shopping outdoors, then New Street is the main shopping thoroughfare with an eclectic mix of shops.

Birmingham's three Bullring markets between them have about 900 stall-holders. The **Indoor Market** sells a diverse range of goods but is best known for its meat and fish section. The **Open Market** is a lively affair with plenty of bargains, and the **Rag Market** is the best place to buy fabrics, though there are additional stalls selling more general products.

Jewellery with the anchor stamp of the **Birmingham Assay Office** is a very popular purchase. Head out to the workshops of the Jewellery Quarter and browse the shop windows for the best bargains. You could even commission your own unique piece from one of the many designers working there.

Many of Birmingham's suburbs have their own colourful markets and shops. These are more culturally diverse, selling goods from around the world; notably Asia, the Caribbean and Eastern Europe.

◯ *The redeveloped Bullring offers excellent shopping*

Eating & drinking

With 25 per cent of the city's population from ethnic minorities, Birmingham's diverse mix of restaurants is a wonderful reflection of this. In the city centre alone it is claimed you can

⬥ *Enjoy canalside dining and a diverse cuisine*

sample 27 different world cuisines. Alongside Thai, Chinese, Indian, Malaysian and continental restaurants are a host of new fusion restaurants that bring together the cuisine of two or more cultures.

For Chinese and other oriental restaurants, as well as a couple of specialist supermarkets, head towards the Chinese Quarter and the adjacent Arcadian complex with its attractive piazza. For Japanese, continental and good food 'on the go', head for the Convention Quarter, in particular Brindleyplace and the canals around Gas Street Basin.

Birmingham has long been known as the Curry Capital of Britain and since the 1970s as the Balti Capital. Introduced by Birmingham's sizeable Kashmiri population, the balti is best tasted in the area between Sparkbrook and Moseley, which has become known as the 'Balti Triangle' because of the high concentration of balti houses located there – currently over 50.

If there is an ethnic group in Birmingham, you will find a restaurant serving that culture's cuisine. Many of the ethnic groups will have their own shops and markets selling the ingredients for their particular dishes. For more traditional home-grown ingredients, the monthly farmers' market on New Street is the best place to buy fresh, often organic, produce.

Generally, lunch is served between 12.00 and 14.30, and dinner from 19.00 onwards. However, many places will serve food from the moment they open. Breakfast too is available at many cafés around the centre and the Convention Quarter.

Entertainment

Whether it is a rock concert at one of Birmingham's world-class venues or a street performer in the Bullring, the city has something for every taste. With the youngest city population in Europe Birmingham's clubs and nightlife are full of energy. However, if your style is cool and sophisticated, then you will find plenty of that too.

Broad Street has the greatest concentration of bars and exciting DJ-fuelled nightclubs and is the *de facto* centre for an energetic night out. The Arcadian and its surrounding area is clubland, and for something more sophisticated and cool, **The Mailbox** is a favourite nightspot. Right next door, The Cube promises to add to the vibe.

You can find live music in the Jewellery Quarter, mostly centred around St Paul's Square. **The Jam House**, whose musical director is none other than Jools Holland, is the magnet that draws people here.

Lovers of ballet, opera and West End shows should check out what's on at the Hippodrome. For more classical theatre there's The Rep, The Old Rep and The Alexandra theatres. Concert-goers have two world-class venues to choose from at either end of Centenary Square, at one end the Symphony Hall and at the other, separated only by road from the square, the Town Hall.

For comedy-lovers, Birmingham has comedy bars aplenty. For film buffs, the multiplex cinema at Star City, the Odeon on New Street or the IMAX at Millennium Point all offer mainstream films. Art house films are shown at the Midlands Art Centre and a more eclectic mix at the Electric Cinema.

During the day there are often street performers in the Bullring or along New Street, and in the summer months they can also be found in some of the many squares. Free lunchtime recitals are also held in several venues around the city. **Rush Hour Blues** takes this concept to a different time and contributes towards easing Birmingham's notorious traffic headaches. This free jazz and blues event is held every Friday between 17.30 and 19.00 in the foyer of Symphony Hall (you can find out who's playing by going to Ⓦ www.birminghamjazz.co.uk and clicking on 'Events').

One of the best ways to find out what's going on and where is to grab a copy of *Area*, Birmingham's What's On monthly publication. Or visit Ⓦ www.areamagazine.wordpress.com

◓ *One of the finest in the world, Birmingham's Symphony Hall*

Sport & relaxation

Birmingham has played an important role in the history of sport. Aston Villa's director in 1888 wrote to his fellow directors suggesting a league of 10 or 12 of the most prominent football clubs in the country. As a result, England became one of the first countries to have a football league competition.

The modern game of tennis was developed in Birmingham with the Edgbaston Archery and Lawn Tennis Society becoming the world's first tennis club.

SPECTATOR SPORTS

Alexander Stadium

This world-class athletics stadium is home to the Birchfield Harriers, one of the country's top athletics clubs.

The Belfry

Its championship courses have hosted the Ryder Cup and other prestigious golf tournaments.

Edgbaston County Cricket Ground

Home to Warwickshire County Cricket Club, this cricket ground hosts international test matches and one-day internationals.

Edgbaston Priory Club

Two of England's Wimbledon singles champions came from this club, which hosts an international tennis tournament in June each year.

National Indoor Arena (NIA)

Hosts many national, European and world championship events in arena sports.

St Andrews

Home of Birmingham City, which at the time of writing was still holding its own in the football Premier League.

Villa Park

Home to Aston Villa Football Club. Tickets for the big football matches are hard to come by so book well in advance.

PARTICIPATION SPORTS

There are several golf courses within the city boundaries and more just outside. For gym-lovers, there are numerous David Lloyd health and fitness clubs in the city, while the canals and larger parks (particularly Sutton Park) provide wonderful opportunities for walking and cycling.

● *For world sporting championships or concerts, head to the NIA*

Accommodation

From the grand old Victorian dames – refurbished of course – to the chic 21st-century boutique hotels, Birmingham has something to suit all pockets from the backpacker's to the business traveller's.

Expect to pay higher prices in the centre of the city and out at the NEC and airport where convenience costs. Look to the suburbs for less expensive luxury accommodation or check out the business hotels at the weekend when prices can come down quite considerably. There are a number of budget hotels scattered round the periphery of the centre. Some of the chain hotels have more than one property in Birmingham but only a few are mentioned in the listing below. A quick look on their website will usually reveal where others close by can be found.

For more accommodation listings see the Visit Birmingham website (Ⓦ www.visitbirmingham.com).

HOSTELS & HOTELS

Birmingham Central Backpackers £ A hostel run by travellers for travellers. There are both dorm and private rooms on offer, and bed and breakfast or half board (buffet dinner) is available. Located not far from the Central Coach Station in Digbeth or Moor Street Station in the city centre. Ⓐ 58 Coventry Street, Digbeth Ⓣ 0121 643 0033
Ⓦ http://birminghamcentralbackpackers.com

Etap Hotel Birmingham Central £ This low-cost chain hotel is a short distance from the ICC and the city centre stations.

ⓐ 1 Great Colmore Street ⓣ 0121 622 7575 ⓕ 0121 622 7576
ⓦ www.etaphotel.com

Ibis Birmingham Centre ££ This affordable hotel is close to the
bars and clubs of The Arcadian and the Chinese Quarter as well
as being convenient for the shops and markets of the Bullring.
The hotel bar serves snacks 24 hours a day. ⓐ Ladywell Walk
ⓣ 0121 622 6010 ⓦ www.ibishotel.com

Plough and Harrow Hotel ££ This three-star Victorian red brick
hotel with 44 en suite rooms follows in a long tradition of
hostelries. There has been an inn or hotel on this site in
Edgbaston since 1612. ⓐ 135 Hagley Road, Edgbaston
ⓣ 0121 454 4111 ⓕ 0121 454 1868
ⓦ www.ploughandharrowhotel.co.uk

Premier Inn ££ In an enviable location in the middle of
Birmingham beside the canal, the Broad Street Premier Inn is
also close to the ICC, Symphony Hall and Brindleyplace. There is
free parking on site. ⓐ 20 Bridge Street ⓣ 0871 527 8078
ⓕ 0871 527 8079 ⓦ www.premierinn.com

Hampton Manor £££ This restored 19th-century manor in
Solihull on the edge of Birmingham was once home to the son
of Prime Minister Robert Peel. It is now a small, 12-bedroomed
luxury hotel. Set in 18 hectares (45 acres) of woodland and
gardens, it is a haven of rest but still with convenient access to
both the city centre and the NEC. ⓐ Shadowbrook Lane, Solihull
ⓣ 01675 446080 ⓦ www.hamptonmanor.eu

Hotel du Vin £££ This luxury hotel, once the Birmingham
Eye Hospital, is the largest belonging to this select chain.
It still retains some of its original early Victorian features, such
as the grand staircase. The 66 rooms and suites are around a
central courtyard; there is a bistro, spa and gym to enjoy. The
hotel is close to the Jewellery Quarter. ⓐ 25 Church Street
ⓣ 0121 200 0600 ⓦ www.hotelduvin.com/hotels/birmingham/
hotel-information

Malmaison Hotel £££ The Malmaison is in The Mailbox, once the
Royal Mail's sorting office for Birmingham. With their chic
chocolate, écru and cream décor, the rooms ooze opulence.
The hotel is noted for its excellent wines and brasserie.
Convenient for the city and the ICC. ⓐ The Mailbox,
Wharfside Street ⓣ 0121 246 5000
ⓦ www.malmaison-birmingham.com

Radisson Blu Hotel £££ Situated midway between the ICC and
the city centre, the Radisson Blu Hotel offers luxury rooms and
suites, along with an award-winning Italian restaurant and, on
the 18th floor, the Obsession Spa, with great views of the city.
ⓐ 12 Holloway Circus, Queensway ⓣ 0121 654 6000
ⓦ www.birmingham.radissonsas.com

APARTMENTS & SELF-CATERING
Back to Backs ££ For something a little different, try one of the
three back-to-back cottages available on a self-catering basis. All
are fitted with modern conveniences and are close to the city
centre and the bars and clubs of The Arcadian complex.

ⓐ 50–54 Inge Street ⓣ 0121 622 2442
ⓦ www.nationaltrustcottages.co.uk

City Nites ££ Spacious and stylish, these luxury serviced
apartments are situated close to the National Indoor Arena. A
room-service continental breakfast is available, while groceries,
chocolates or flowers can be delivered on request.
ⓐ Arena View, Edward Street ⓣ 0121 233 1155
ⓦ www.city-nites.com

The Spires £££ Newly built spacious serviced apartments with
maid service and continental breakfast. One- or two-bedroomed
apartments and de-luxe suites are available for short- or long-
term stays. They are close to the canals and The Mailbox and
within easy walking distance of the ICC and the city centre.
ⓐ 10 Commercial Street ⓣ 0845 270 0090
ⓦ www.thespires.co.uk

Staying Cool £££ Individually designed serviced apartments in
the Rotunda right above the Bullring. All apartments come with
a large flat-screen TV, Apple computer, iPod docks and WiFi. The
fully equipped kitchen has a Gaggia espresso maker.
ⓐ Rotunda, 150 New Street ⓣ 0121 643 0815
ⓦ www.stayingcool.com

THE BEST OF BIRMINGHAM

Below are a selection of places to visit, things to do and places to eat that will give a feel for the best Birmingham has to offer.

TOP 10 ATTRACTIONS

- **Thinktank** at Millennium Point is a hands-on interactive science museum with a planetarium (see pages 47).

- **Brindleyplace** is the place to go for a bite to eat at one of the restaurants situated beside the canal (see page 58).

- **Symphony Hall** Home to the City of Birmingham Symphony Orchestra, the hall's acoustics are said to be among the best in the world (see page 68).

- **Shop till you drop** at the Bullring shopping centre, the Pavilions and the Victorian arcades – and The Mailbox if you have the stamina (see pages 14–15).

- **Birmingham Museum and Art Gallery** contains the largest collection of Pre-Raphaelite paintings in the world (see pages 51–2).

- The **Back to Backs** are a wonderfully preserved courtyard of houses built in the 19th century for Birmingham's rapidly expanding population (see page 45).

- The **Museum of the Jewellery Quarter** gives an insight into the workings of a jewellery workshop (see page 61).

- The **Balti Triangle** is a mecca for curry fans. There are over 50 balti houses in this small area between Sparkbrook and Moseley (see page 17).

- **Cannon Hill Park** is lovely for a stroll in spring or summer; it's a flower-lover's paradise (see page 73).

- The **Custard Factory**, once the site of Bird's Custard production, is now home to a bohemian art community, with art studios, galleries, independent shops and cafés (see page 46).

❥ *A tranquil canal scene amid the bustle of city life*

Suggested itineraries

HALF-DAY: BIRMINGHAM IN A HURRY

Follow the canal from The Mailbox, through Gas Street Basin to
Brindleyplace. Grab yourself a canalside snack and drink or visit
the Ikon Gallery before crossing the canal and going through
the International Convention Centre. Then cross Centenary
Square and head for the Birmingham Museum and Art Gallery
(BMAG). Step inside and have a quick look at the collection of
Pre-Raphaelite paintings before speed shopping down New
Street to the Bullring and St Martin's in the Bullring to see the
stunning architecture of the Selfridges building.

1 DAY: TIME TO SEE A LITTLE MORE

Add to the half-day itinerary a tour of the Back to Backs before
taking the tram from Snow Hill Station to the Jewellery Quarter
and visiting the Museum of the Jewellery Quarter. Then spend
some time wandering around the unique jewellery shops and
design studios. If you're lucky, you might even pick up a choice
piece of costume jewellery or a more contemporary item.

2–3 DAYS: SHORT CITY-BREAK

Having more time to play with you can enjoy the Birmingham
Museum and Art Gallery at a leisurely pace and have a relaxing
lunch at Brindleyplace. Spend half a day at Thinktank and the
Planetarium before paying a visit to the Custard Factory. You can
fill another day by venturing further out of the city: there's
Cadbury World in Bournville or the Botanical Gardens and the
Barber Institute of Fine Arts in Edgbaston.

LONGER: ENJOYING BIRMINGHAM TO THE FULL

Now you really can enjoy yourself! Why not take a long walk in Sutton Park, stroll in Cannon Hill Park or amble along the city's canals. You could also visit some of Birmingham's historic buildings. Try Soho House, the home of Matthew Boulton, one of the 18th-century founders of the influential Lunar Society. Alternatively, head for the tranquil Sarehole Mill, where J R R Tolkien spent his childhood, or immerse yourself in English history by wandering through the magnificent house and grounds of Aston Hall. Further afield, consider having a day out at Warwick Castle, or why not take the steam-hauled Shakespeare Express to Stratford-upon-Avon. And then there's Dudley for its zoo or the Black Country Living Museum.

🔺 *The Mailbox is home to exclusive shops and restaurants*

Something for nothing

Birmingham is awash with museums where entry is free. Entry to the Birmingham Museum and Art Gallery (BMAG), the Barber Institute of Fine Arts, the Ikon Gallery, St Paul's Gallery and the Custard Factory will cost you nothing.

Other sites, notably those under the auspices of the BMAG, also have a policy of free admission. These include Soho House, Aston Hall, Blakesley Hall and Sarehole Mill. In the Jewellery Quarter both the Museum of the Jewellery Quarter and The Pen Room will not cost you a penny to visit.

Birmingham is blessed with numerous parks that provide ample opportunity for walking, cycling or simply escaping from the city's busy shops and bustling streets. Sutton Park is ideal for the more country feel, Cannon Hill Park for the more urban feel. Likewise, you can stroll or cycle along the canal paths of the city for free.

THE SOUND OF MUSIC
There are often free music recitals and performances around the city, ranging from classical music to jazz to church music. Check the church noticeboards and ask at the tourist office for details of what's on.

When it rains

Since many of Birmingham's attractions are indoors or under cover, a rainy day should not prevent you from having an enjoyable trip. Shopping in the Bullring shopping centre and/or the nearby Pavilions will keep you dry and happily occupied for hours. Alternatively, the Indoor Market is a good place to seek shelter.

Birmingham has a plethora of museums and galleries that can be saved for the inevitable rainy day. The Birmingham Museum and Art Gallery and the Ikon Gallery in the centre, and the Museum of the Jewellery Quarter and the Barber Institute of Fine Arts a little further out, are all excellent places to seek cover and culture.

If the wet weather persists, the science museum Thinktank will take up at least half a day if you include a visit to the Planetarium, and catching a film at the large IMAX Cinema in the same building could help fill the other half. If you have children to amuse, try Star City. Aimed at families, this leisure complex has bowling alleys, adventure golf, an indoor climbing centre and vast cinemas.

If you're driving, try heading out to Cadbury World in Bournville or the National Sea Life Centre in Brindleyplace – you'll easily stay entertained – and dry – for a whole day.

On arrival

ARRIVING
By air

Birmingham International Airport connects to over 100 cities and is served by 50 airlines, including 7 budget airlines. It is well connected to central Birmingham and is adjacent to the National Exhibition Centre. However, there are no flights connecting London and Birmingham.

A link service runs every two minutes between the airport and Birmingham International railway station, where services to the city centre run up to seven times an hour. There's a taxi rank outside the airport, but expect to pay around £25 if you wish to take a taxi to the city centre. As to bus services, the 900 Airport Link runs every 20 minutes between the terminals and the city centre. You will need the exact fare for the bus.

All the major car hire firms have desks at the airport.
Avis ☏ 0844 544 6013
Budget ☏ 0844 544 4602
Enterprise ☏ 0121 782 9030
Europcar ☏ 0121 782 6507
Hertz ☏ 0870 846 0008
National ☏ 0121 782 5481

By rail

The city is a major hub of Britain's rail network, with the majority of trains arriving and departing from one station, New Street. The two other stations, Moor Street and Snow Hill, have far fewer services. New Street Station is very busy, so listen carefully to announcements and check the information monitors to make sure you board the right train.

There are two or more trains an hour arriving at New Street Station from Bristol, South Wales, Scotland, Manchester, Liverpool, Oxford and Sheffield. The most frequent train service is from London Euston.

Moor Street Station is served by a slower, less expensive service from London's Marylebone Station and the train follows a different route. Snow Hill Station on the same line is also the terminus for the Metro tram that runs to Wolverhampton through the Jewellery Quarter.

By coach

All intercity coaches use Digbeth Central Coach Station, which was completed early in 2010. Access from here to the city centre is easy. Megabus (London only) and National Express are the main operators providing intercity coach links with Birmingham. There are half-hourly services (sometimes more frequent) to central London. Services to other major cities are less frequent but there is usually one every two hours or less.

National Express also runs services that connect major airports. There are direct and frequent coach services between London's Gatwick and Heathrow (Terminal 5) airports and Birmingham International Airport.

By road

All roads lead to Birmingham, it seems. The city is surrounded by a motorway network from where you can head out in almost

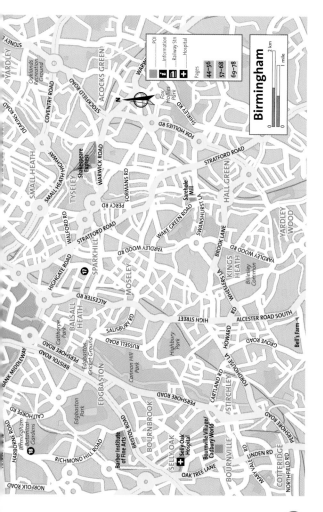

Birmingham

Pages
44–56
57–68
69–78

POI
Information
Railway Stn
Hospital

0 — 2 km
0 — 1 mile

35

every direction. The M5, M6 and M42 form the ring of motorways around the city. The M50 and M54 a short distance away connect the city with South Wales and North Wales respectively, and the M40 near Solihull provides an alternative, less congested route to London. In addition, several major trunk roads fill in the gaps left by the motorway network. The country's biggest road interchange, Spaghetti Junction, is on the M6 north of the city centre.

Despite being the city of the car, it is not easy to drive or park in the centre of Birmingham. A motorway link road, the A38(M), takes traffic from the M6 at Spaghetti Junction directly into the city centre. The 15,000 parking spaces here are at a premium but many city centre hotels have special deals for their guests arriving by car. When driving into or around Birmingham, try to avoid the rush hours (07.30–09.30 and 16.00–18.30).

FINDING YOUR FEET

It is possible to walk from Eastside to the Convention Quarter without having to dodge traffic, as most of the centre of Birmingham is pedestrianised. Follow the network of canal paths and you can get to places much further afield whilst avoiding traffic. Apart from a few service roads and one to New Street Station, traffic is absent from the very centre of Birmingham.

The city centre is relatively crime free and although some places appear run down there is less to fear than one would think. You can expect some overzealous boisterousness along Broad Street when the clubs and bars empty out from 23.00 onwards. Elsewhere, use a little common sense and take the usual precautions, and you should have no problem.

ORIENTATION

Visitors arriving in the city centre will notice two obvious and iconic landmarks: the first is the **Rotunda**, the tall circular building near the Bullring, and the second is the **Selfridges** building, with its audacious curves and distinctive aluminium disc covering. Either one or the other of these is visible from most of the central areas and makes orientation relatively easy. Just a little further out, the dark glass tower of the Hyatt Regency hotel, the blue-glassed Radisson Blu Hotel and the BT Tower are all recognisable landmarks to aid the visitor when exploring Birmingham's central areas.

⬤ *The attractive Moor Street Station*

New Street is the main shopping thoroughfare and runs from the Bullring to Victoria Square where the Convention Quarter begins. Broad Street, a continuation of New Street, is where to head for the city's buzzing nightlife and can be reached along the canals from The Mailbox or the National Indoor Arena. Newhall Street near St Phillip's Square will take you to the heart of the Jewellery Quarter, while Pershore Street leads you into the Chinese Quarter.

GETTING AROUND

Network West Midlands operates all the public transport services in the city, including the bus, train and Metro.

Bus

The city's largest bus company is Travel West Midlands, with almost 600 routes. There is no central bus station but most services can be caught at one of four principal streets (Colmore Row, Bull Street, Corporation Street or Stephenson Street). There are two circular bus routes – the inner and outer circle (Nos 8 and 11 respectively). Most other services radiate out from the city centre. For more information on routes or to download route maps, check out the Travel West Midlands website Ⓦ www.travelwm.co.uk or telephone the information line on ☎ 0871 200 2233 between 07.00 and 21.30.

Bus tickets can be purchased from the bus driver and you must have the correct change. Alternatively, you can buy a one-day travel card for around £5, which allows unlimited travel on the buses, trains and Metro. These can be purchased from the bus driver or at railway stations.

◯ *The Selfridges building is a stunning focal point*

Train

There is a good local rail network to destinations in Birmingham and the West Midlands in addition to intercity services across Britain. There are three stations in the centre: New Street, Moor Street and, in the business district, Snow Hill, all with local services.

Local fares range from around £1.50 to £6.00 for an off-peak return. Tickets must be bought before boarding the train either from the ticket office or from machines on the platforms. You can purchase standard day singles and standard day returns, available for travel at any time, or cheap day returns for travel after 09.30 Monday to Friday. There are also day passes and weekly passes that allow travel on the entire Network West Midlands line.

Taxi

There are two types of taxi: the black cabs that can pick up fares anywhere, and private taxis that must be pre-booked.

▶ *Old meets new in Birmingham's thriving centre*

 # THE CITY OF
Birmingham

Introduction to city areas

Central Birmingham is very easy to get around on foot, with a high concentration of things to see and do in a relatively small area. There is also a great deal to see in the region of Greater Birmingham, but these attractions are spread out over a much wider – and greener – area.

For the purposes of the guide, the central area is divided into two sections described as **City Centre East** and **City Centre West**. City Centre East is the area east of Bristol Street and Corporation Street and includes the Eastside, where you will find Aston University, Millennium Point, the Chinese Quarter and the central shopping areas. City Centre West is the area that lies west of that line, and includes the Jewellery Quarter and the Convention Quarter.

Outside the Centre describes those areas of Birmingham that lie beyond the A4540 'middle ring road', or 'middleway'. Many of these districts were once towns in their own right but have since been swallowed up by the ever-expanding city. It is in this area where you will find some of the beautiful parks and fine houses that hark back to a pre-industrial past.

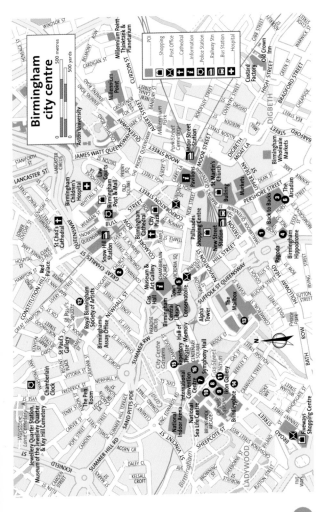

City centre east

For the purposes of this guide, the central area is divided into two: **City Centre East** and **City Centre West**. City Centre East has three distinct areas: **Eastside**, filled with centres of learning, technology and entertainment and the original manufacturing base of the city; the **Chinese Quarter**, which is so much more than a district of Chinese restaurants; and the **central shopping area**, which is the commercial and retail hub of the city and is largely pedestrianised.

Eastside is a district currently under construction. Ambitious development plans are turning the area into a centre for technology and learning, with a healthy mix of educational entertainment in places like Millennium Point. Aston University has always been here but other educational establishments such as the Matthew Boulton College have relocated or established their campuses here. With a high density of students and young techno entrepreneurs living or working here, Eastside has a vibrant buzz all of its own.

The **central shopping area** is where the huge redesigned and rebuilt Bullring shopping centre is located, along with the indoor and outdoor markets, other shopping areas and Birmingham's civic buildings. This part of the city was heavily damaged during the Blitz and as a result redbrick Victorian buildings sit cheek by jowl with the concrete blocks of the 1960s and 70s and the glass and metal edifices of the late 20th and early 21st centuries.

The **Chinese Quarter**, as its name suggests, is where Chinese immigrants have settled and opened businesses. During Chinese New Year, the wonderfully colourful and vibrant celebrations are as good as any seen in the Chinatowns of London or Manchester. Come March, however, and the festivities take on a distinctly Irish flavour as the city's residents celebrate St Patrick's Day in this part of town. The Chinese Quarter is also home to the Birmingham Hippodrome and the widely acclaimed Birmingham Royal Ballet.

SIGHTS & ATTRACTIONS

Back to backs

This restored 19th-century courtyard has 11 back-to-back houses. These back to backs were common in Birmingham, as the influx of people during the Industrial Revolution meant there was a chronic need for cheap housing. One in four residents in Birmingham lived in housing similar to these. During the slum clearances of the 1960s, most were demolished but these were still in use until 1977. The houses have been set up to show four different periods between 1840 and 1977. Three houses are available as holiday cottages. Don't miss the traditional sweet shop on the corner that sells sweets in jars. ⓐ Inge Street/Hurst Street ⓐ 0121 666 7671 ⓦ www.nationaltrust.org.uk ⓔ backtobacks@nationaltrust.org.uk ⓛ 10.00–17.00 Tues–Sun, closed Mon except Bank Holidays (Feb–Dec) ⓝ Bus: 61, 62, 63, 144 ⓘ Admission with charge-timed ticket and guided tour only. Booking advised

Chamberlain Square

This majestic square was designed and built to commemorate Joseph Chamberlain, father of Prime Minister Neville Chamberlain.

In the centre of the square is a fountain and the neo-Gothic Chamberlain Memorial, while reclining on the steps of the Birmingham Central Library is a bronze statue of Thomas Attwood, the 19th-century economist. The annual German Christmas Market is held here. Ⓝ Bus: 9, 21, 22, 23, 24, 120, 126, 140, 141, 192

Custard Factory

It was in this factory that the pharmacist Alfred Bird developed the egg-less custard that many Britons know and love. Today, the building houses an eclectic mix of media and arts professionals. This rather bohemian community is complemented by chic bars, trendy cafés, dance studios, galleries and shops. During the summer a weekly flea market is held here on a Sunday, with artists, designers, street entertainers, children's activities and food stalls. ⓐ Gibb Street ① 0121 224 7777 Ⓦ www.custardfactory.co.uk ⓔ info@custardfactory.co.uk ⓛ 07.00–21.00 Mon–Fri, 07.00–21.30 Sat & Sun Ⓝ Bus: 6, 37, 50, 57, 57A, 58, 60, 96

Law Courts

The Law Courts are the finest example of Victorian redbrick and terracotta decoration in Birmingham. Queen Victoria laid the foundation stone in 1887 and her statue graces the top of the entrance porch. ⓐ Steelhouse Lane ⓛ 09.00–17.00 Mon–Fri, closed Sat & Sun Ⓝ Bus: 115, 116

Millennium Point

This huge building covers the area of six football pitches and houses the IMAX Cinema, the Planetarium and Thinktank.

Chronicling Birmingham's contribution to the world of science and industry, **Thinktank** is a truly fascinating museum. It has over 200 interactive exhibits that challenge visitors to uncover the past, discover the present, and predict the future of science and technology. Lots of hands-on stuff and great fun for all the family. ⓐ Millennium Point, Curzon Street ⓣ 0121 202 2222 ⓦ www.thinktank.ac ⓔ findout@thinktank.ac ⓛ 10.00–17.00 daily ⓝ Train: Moor Street; Bus: 14, 27, 55 ⓘ Admission charge

Inside Thinktank is the **Planetarium**, where a digital projection onto a dome screen takes visitors on a mesmerising journey through the universe in high definition. ⓐ Millennium Point, Curzon Street ⓣ 0121 202 2222 ⓦ www.thinktank.ac ⓔ findout@thinktank.ac ⓛ 10.00–17.00 daily ⓝ Train: Moor Street; Bus: 14, 27, 55 ⓘ Admission charge in addition to entry into Thinktank

Moor Street Station

A grade II listed building, this recently refurbished Edwardian station was built in 1909 by the Great Western Railway.

Old Crown Inn

Situated next door to the Custard Factory, this historic building is one of the few surviving half-timbered houses in Birmingham. Dating back to the 14th century, the Old Crown Inn still serves food and drink. Bed and breakfast accommodation is also available. ⓐ 188 High Street, Deritend ⓣ 0121 248 1368 ⓦ www.theoldcrown.com ⓛ During licensing hours ⓝ Train: Bordesley; Bus: 37, 50, 57, 57A, 58, 60, 96

Pagoda

This gift to Birmingham from its most prominent Chinese businessman is placed in a small garden in the centre of Smallbrook Queensway roundabout. ⓐ Smallbrook Queensway Ⓝ Bus: 61, 62, 63, 143, 144, 146

St Chad's Cathedral

Completed in 1841, the neo-Gothic St Chad's was the first Roman Catholic cathedral to be built in Britain after the Reformation. ⓐ St Chad's Queensway Ⓣ 0121 230 6201 Ⓕ 0121 230 6279 Ⓦ http://stchadcathedral.org.uk Ⓛ 07.00–17.00 Mon–Fri, 09.00–17.00 Sat, 07.00–15.00 Sun Ⓝ Bus: 7, 16, 46, 74, 79

St Martin in the Bullring

This plaza is an open space with modern sculptures and water features incorporated in the redesign of the Bullring. Its public spaces are often used as venues for performing arts. At the centre stands **St Martin's Church**.

The present church is a late-19th-century Gothic-style building that stands on the site of the oldest church in Birmingham. It was designed by Alfred Chatwin, who also worked on the Houses of Parliament in London. Inside, the window by Pre-Raphaelite artist Edward Burne-Jones is truly magnificent, having miraculously survived the World War II bombing. ⓐ Edgbaston Street Ⓣ 0121 600 6020 Ⓕ 0121 600 6021 Ⓦ www.bullring.org ⓔ info@bullring.org Ⓛ 10.00–16.30 Mon–Sat, 09.00–19.30 Sun Ⓝ Train: Moor Street, New Street; Bus: All buses into the city using the A34 Stratford Road or A45 Coventry Road

St Phillip's Place

A quiet square in the centre of the business district and not far from the shops, St Phillip's Place is surrounded by well-preserved buildings from the 18th and 19th centuries. The Bank of England was once located here in the building that now, ironically, houses the Bank of Scotland. In the centre of the square stands **Birmingham Cathedral**.

🔺 *Lorenzo Quinn's* Tree of Life *commemorates those who died in bombing raids*

In 1905 Birmingham diocese was created and the first bishop chose the English Baroque-style church consecrated in 1715 as his seat. It is worth visiting to see the four stained-glass windows by Edward Burne-Jones. ⓐ Colmore Row
ⓣ 0121 262 1840 ⓦ www.birminghamcathedral.com
ⓔ enquiries@birminghamcathedral.com ⓛ 07.30–17.00 Mon–Fri, 08.30–17.00 Sat & Sun (July–Sept, Easter, Christmas); 07.30–18.30 Mon–Fri, 08.30–17.00 Sat & Sun (Sept–July); ⓝ Train: Snow Hill; Tram: Snow Hill; Bus: All buses to the city centre

Victoria Square

This magnificent square is open and spacious and beloved by Brummies. In front of the Council House is Europe's largest fountain, with a flow of around 3,000 gallons per minute. Officially called the **River**, it is known locally as the 'Floozie in the Jacuzzi' because of the large reclining nude that graces the fountain. The Renaissance-style **Council House** (not open to the public) occupies one side of the square and the **Town Hall** another. The square has a statue of its namesake, **Queen Victoria**, and Antony Gormley's rather controversial **Iron Man**.
ⓝ Bus: 9, 21, 22, 23, 24, 120, 126, 140, 141, 192

CULTURE

Birmingham Central Library

Both loathed and loved, this building was described by Prince Charles as '...an essay in concrete "brutalism"'. Europe's largest library, it has a memorial room dedicated to Shakespeare's early folio editions. As part of the city's redevelopment plans, the library

⬤ *The magnificent 19th-century Council House dominates Victoria Square*

is soon to be relocated a few hundred metres away to Centenary Square, and the plans to demolish the current building are in a state of flux. ⓐ Paradise Circus ❶ 0121 303 4511 ⓦ www.birmingham.gov.uk ⏱ 09.00–20.00 Mon–Fri, 09.00–17.00 Sat, closed Sun ⓝ Bus: 9, 21, 22, 23, 24, 120, 126, 140, 141, 192

Birmingham Museum and Art Gallery (BMAG)

This art gallery, housed in a beautiful Victorian building, contains the largest collection of Pre-Raphaelite paintings in the world. Its diverse collection of over 500,000 objects is expertly displayed in over 40 galleries. ⓐ Chamberlain Square

📞 0121 303 2834 🌐 www.bmag.org.uk
✉ bmag_enquiries@birmingham.gov.uk 🕐 10.00–17.00 Mon–
Thur & Sat, 10.30–17.00 Fri, 12.30–17.00 Sun 🚌 Bus: 9, 21, 22, 23, 24,
120, 126, 140, 141, 192

Millennium Point – IMAX Cinema

With its 22 x 16 m (72 x 52ft 6in) wide screen, this was the first
IMAX and largest cinema to be built in the West Midlands.
Using IMAX® 3D technology, the cinema brings a whole new
3D experience to viewers. 📍 Millennium Point, Curzon Street
📞 0121 202 2222 🌐 www.imax.ac ✉ findout@thinktank.ac
🕐 10.00–17.00 daily 🚊 Train: Moor Street; Bus: 14, 27, 55
❗ Admission charge

RETAIL THERAPY

Bullring markets There has been a market in the Bullring
since 1154. Today, there are three markets opened to the
public, with nearly 900 stalls. The **Indoor Market** is known for
its meat and fish though there is a diverse range of other
goods on sale. The **Open Market** is the place to find bargains
for just about anything, and the **Rag Market** has a diverse
range of goods for sale but is best known for its huge range
of fabrics – hence the name. Open Market 🕐 09.00–17.00
Tues–Sat, closed Sun & Mon. Indoor Market 🕐 09.00–17.30
Mon–Sat, closed Sun. Rag Market 📍 Edgbaston Street
📞 0121 464 8349 🌐 www.ragmarket.com
✉ marketstalls@birmingham.gov.uk
🕐 09.00–17.00 Tues & Thur–Sat, closed Mon, Wed & Sun

Bullring shopping centre The Bullring is an ambitious redevelopment of the original Bull Ring built in the late 1960s, once the largest covered shopping centre outside the USA. It includes the futuristic architecture of **Selfridges**. Constructed of 15,000 aluminium discs, it is a design that has won international acclaim and criticism and has been described as 'space fungus' and dubbed the 'Armadillo' by locals. Inside, the 140 shops, cafés and restaurants feature most of the big-name high-street retailers. ⓐ Bullring ⓣ 0121 632 1526 ⓦ www.bullring.co.uk ⓛ 09.30–20.00 Mon–Fri, 09.00–20.00 Sat, 11.00–17.00 Sun ⓝ Train: Moor Street, New Street; Bus: All services to city centre stop within five minutes' walk of the Bullring

Great Western Arcade This is the most impressive of the city's Victorian shopping arcades, which has now been restored to its former state and is home to a number of boutique shops and independent retailers. Originally built in 1874 over the tunnel of the Great Western Railway, it was faithfully restored after bomb damage in World War II. ⓐ Colmore Row ⓣ 0121 236 5417 ⓕ 0121 236 5417 ⓦ www.greatwesternarcade.co.uk ⓛ 09.00–18.00 Mon–Wed & Sat, 09.00–20.00 Thur & Fri, 11.00–17.00 Sun ⓝ All buses to the city

Pallasades This shopping centre contains around 90 shops and, located just above Birmingham's main railway station, is conveniently situated for shoppers visiting the city from further afield. ⓐ Above New Street Station ⓣ 0121 633 3070 ⓦ www.thepallasades.co.uk ⓛ 09.00–18.00 Mon–Sat, 10.00–17.00 Sun ⓝ Train: New Street Station; Bus: Most buses to the city

Pavilions Adjacent to the Bullring, this shopping centre has four floors of well-known high-street names. The top floor houses the Food Loft. ⓐ 38 High Street ⓣ 0121 631 4121 ⓦ www.pavilionsshopping.com ⓛ 09.30–18.00 Mon–Wed, Fri & Sat; 09.30–19.00 Thur, 11.00–17.00 Sun ⓝ Train: New Street, Snow Hill; Tram: Snow Hill; Bus: All buses into the city

TAKING A BREAK

Chung Ying Garden ££ ❶ The largest Chinese restaurant in Birmingham in the heart of the Chinese Quarter. The clubs and bars of The Arcadian and the Birmingham Hippodrome are close by. The wonderfully varied menu has 450 dishes to choose from. ⓐ 17 Thorp Street ⓣ 0121 666 6622 ⓦ www.chungying.co.uk ⓝ Bus: 61, 62, 63, 144

Opus £££ ❷ A restaurant committed to using only locally sourced, and in-season, ingredients in a creative way. ⓐ 54 Cornwall Street ⓣ 0121 200 2323 ⓦ www.opusrestaurant.co.uk ⓝ Train: Snow Hill; Tram: Snow Hill; Bus: 101

AFTER DARK

Bar & restaurant
Poppy Red and Restaurant £ ❸ Bar with post-Soviet-bloc-style décor and excellent food. DJs play a mix of music for dancing late into the night after dinner. ⓐ The Arcadian ⓣ 0121 687 1200 ⓦ www.poppy-red.com ⓔ info@poppy-red.com ⓝ Bus: 2, 3, 5, 6, 35, 45

Theatre & concert hall

Birmingham Hippodrome ❹ Completed in 1899, the Hippodrome is Birmingham's oldest surviving theatre. Recently refurbished, the theatre has a new entrance with bars and restaurants. The glass façade hides the interior of the actual theatre, which has been preserved in all its elegance. It's home to the Birmingham Royal Ballet company (which prior to relocating to Birmingham was known as the Sadler's Wells Royal Ballet) and DanceXchange, and hosts the Birmingham International Dance Festival. It is also the preferred venue for the Welsh National Opera. ⓐ Hurst Street ⓣ Box office: 0844 338 5000 ⓦ www.birminghamhippodrome.com ⓛ Performance days: 10.00–20.00 daily; non-performance days: 10.00–18.00 daily ⓝ Bus: 61, 62, 63, 144

Town Hall ❺ Based on the ancient Temple of Castor and Pollux in Rome, Birmingham's Town Hall has some of the best

🔺 *The Arcadian has a distinctly Chinese flavour*

acoustics in the city. The auditorium seats 4,000 people and was once home to the City of Birmingham Symphony Orchestra (CBSO). ⓐ Victoria Square ⓣ Box office: 0121 780 3333 ⓦ www.thsh.co.uk ⓔ Box office: boxoffice@thsh.co.uk Ⓝ Bus: 9, 120, 126, 140, 141, 192

Entertainment complex

The Arcadian ❶ A doughnut-shaped complex containing bars and restaurants set around a spacious piazza in the Chinese Quarter. You'll also find a few Chinese supermarkets here. It's great for alfresco dining, as well as for pre- and post-theatre drinks if you've got tickets for a ballet, play or show at the Hippodrome across the road. ⓐ Hurst Street ⓣ 0121 622 5348 ⓦ www.thearcadian.co.uk Ⓝ Bus: 2, 5, 6, 35, 45, 178

❶ Dhruva Mistry's River *adorns the fountain in Victoria Square*

City centre west

This area has two distinct districts: the Convention Quarter and the Jewellery Quarter. The **Convention Quarter** is where The International Convention Centre (ICC), Symphony Hall and the National Indoor Arena (NIA) are all located. Serving these are the bars, restaurants, clubs and cafés along the renovated canals and Broad Street.

To the northwest of the city centre is the **Jewellery Quarter**. Birmingham has always been famous for its metalworking industry and the jewellery trades grew out of this abundance of metalworking skills – 40 per cent of jewellery sold in Britain is made in Birmingham. The **JQ**, as it is often known, is easily reached on foot or by the Metro tram and is the place to go for designer jewellery at prices below those on the high street. There are several trails leading round the quarter, each one marked with easy-to-follow plaques in the pavement.

SIGHTS & ATTRACTIONS

Birmingham Assay Office

The Birmingham Assay Office was founded in 1773 after lobbying by the great industrialist Matthew Boulton resulted in the Hallmarks Act. Today, it hallmarks over 12 million articles a year and is the largest assay office in the world. Tours can be booked in advance to see the Silver Collection. The assay mark for Birmingham is the anchor. ⓐ Newhall Street ⓣ 0871 871 6020 ⓕ 0121 236 9032 ⓦ www.theassayoffice.co.uk ⓛ 08.30–16.00 Mon–Thur, 08.30–15.00 Fri, closed Sat & Sun

Brindleyplace

Brindleyplace is the regenerated Birmingham's pride and joy. Named after the man who built the adjacent Birmingham and Wolverhampton Canal, it has a diverse range of building styles and some preserved buildings thrown into the mix. Somehow it all works and has won the International Excellence on the Waterfront Award, putting it up there with the likes of New York, Sydney Harbour and Boston. There are dozens of cafés and restaurants around its squares and along the canalside. A bridge connects Brindleyplace with the ICC, making it an ideal place to eat post-concert or convention. Ⓝ Bus: 1, 9, 10, 22, 24, 29, 120, 126, 128

🔺 *Take a tour of Birmingham Assay Office*

Cemeteries

Key Hill Cemetery was the first in Birmingham and is the final resting place of the great politician Joseph Chamberlain. **Warstone Lane Cemetery** has some interesting catacombs and is where the printer John Baskerville, who invented the typeface that bears his name, is buried. ⓐ Vyse Street Ⓝ Train: Jewellery Quarter; Tram: Jewellery Quarter; Bus: 8A, 8C, 101

Centenary Square

Centenary Square on Broad Street is one of the city's newest squares, named in 1989 to commemorate 100 years of Birmingham's status as a city. Its open design took over half a million bricks. Symphony Hall (in the ICC), the Rep theatre and Baskerville House around the square are soon to be joined by the new Birmingham City Library. Ⓝ Bus: 1, 9, 10, 22, 24, 29, 120, 126, 128

Chamberlain Clock

Built to commemorate local MP Joseph Chamberlain's visit to South Africa in 1903, this unique landmark is considered the centre of the Jewellery Quarter. ⓐ Vyse Street/Frederick Street Ⓝ Train: Jewellery Quarter; Tram: Jewellery Quarter; Bus: 8A, 101

Gas Street Basin and canals

Birmingham has more miles of canals than Venice. As road and rail took over the city, many fell into disrepair, but have recently been given a new lease of life. Bars, cafés and restaurants, as well as hotels and apartments, have been built or refurbished from the once-derelict warehouses along the banks. Pathways allow pedestrians and cyclists to reach the countryside and suburbs of Birmingham without ever needing to resort to the roads. **Gas Street Basin** is at the centre of the network and right in the middle of the convention district. It's a great place to sit with a drink and enjoy the brightly painted canal boats or take a sightseeing canal boat trip to explore further the city's waterways. ⓐ Gas Street Ⓝ Bus: 1, 9, 10, 22, 24, 29, 120, 126, 128

Hall of Memory

Opened in 1925, this touching memorial to those who died in the two world wars is a large domed building surrounded by statues. There are three books of remembrance on display.
ⓐ Centenary Square Ⓝ Bus: 1, 9, 10, 22, 24, 29, 120, 126, 128

⬥ The rejuvenated Gas Street Basin

🔵 *Learn about Birmingham's jewellery trade*

Museum of the Jewellery Quarter

In 1981 jewellers Smith & Pepper closed its doors, leaving the building just as it was. Tools on the worktops and archives of invoices were left to gather dust. Nine years later Birmingham City Council opened up the building, catalogued the 70,000 items, cleaned up and reopened the workshops as a museum. Guided tours now take you through the workshops and there are demonstrations of how the jewellery was once produced. Displays also give an insight into the history of the jewellery trade in Birmingham. 🅰 75–79 Vyse Street 📞 0121 554 3598 🌐 www.bmag.org.uk 🕐 10.30–16.00 Tues–Sat, closed Sun & Mon except Bank Holidays 🅝 Train: Jewellery Quarter; Tram: Jewellery Quarter; Bus: 8C

National Sea Life Centre

This aquatic centre is not what you would expect to find in Birmingham, which is as far from the sea as it is possible to be in Britain. Experience life beneath the waves with an underwater tunnel through the one million litres of sea water, a touch tank and over 60 other marine displays.

🅐 The Water's Edge, Brindleyplace 🕿 0871 716 2612 🅔 slcbirmingham@merlinentertainments.biz 🕑 10.00–18.00 daily 🅝 Bus: 1, 9, 10, 22, 24, 29, 120, 126, 128 ❶ Admission charge

The Pen Room

Another industry that grew out of the metalworking skills of Birmingham's craftsmen was the invention and manufacture of the pen. For over 100 years Birmingham was the centre of the pen trade, accelerating the development of literacy worldwide. The museum gives an insight into the processes involved in making pens and the employment opportunities the trade gave to thousands of people, especially women.

🅐 Argent Centre, 60 Frederick Street 🕿 0121 236 9834 🅦 www.penroom.co.uk 🅔 pentalk@penroom.co.uk 🕑 11.00–16.00 Mon–Sat, 13.00–16.00 Sun 🅝 Train: Jewellery Quarter; Tram: Jewellery Quarter; Bus: 101

Red Palace

Built in 1896 as a memorial to the Commander in Chief of the British Empire, Lord Roberts of Kandahar, this unusual terracotta building comes to a point rather like the prow of a ship.

🅐 Constitution Hill 🅝 Bus: 16, 46, 74, 79

St Paul's Square and St Paul's Church

The sole surviving Georgian square in Birmingham is home to
St Paul's Church. This church was modelled on St Martin's-in-
the-Fields, in London's Trafalgar Square, and among the
worshippers here were the novelist Washington Irving, and
engineers James Watt and Matthew Boulton. ❷ St Paul's Square
❶ 0121 236 7858 ❶ 12.00–14.30 Mon–Fri, closed Sat & Sun
🚊 Tram: St Paul's; Bus: 101

❍ St Paul's Square is the tranquil setting for this fine church

CULTURE

ICC/Symphony Hall

Although architecturally nothing special on the outside, inside, the International Convention Centre, or ICC, is a stunning collection of meeting places with all the latest cutting-edge technology required for holding conventions of almost any size – from several thousand to just a few. In 1998 the G8 Summit was held here, as was the Eurovision Song Contest. There are a number of works of art in and around the building. The ICC, which has a public right of way through it and hence is open 24 hours a day, also incorporates the **Symphony Hall**, which is the new home of the City of Birmingham Symphony Orchestra (CBSO). **ⓐ** Broad Street/Centenary Square **ⓣ** 0121 200 2000 **ⓦ** www.theicc.co.uk **ⓔ** info@theicc.co.uk **ⓛ** 24 hours daily **ⓝ** Bus: 1, 9, 10, 22, 24, 29, 120, 126, 128 **ⓘ** Free except for entry to events

Ikon Gallery

Among the lawns and fountains of Brindleyplace is the neo-Gothic school building of the Ikon Gallery. It has a reputation for exhibiting innovative contemporary art using all conceivable media. **ⓐ** Oozells Square, Brindleyplace **ⓣ** 0121 248 0708 **ⓦ** www.ikon-gallery.co.uk **ⓛ** 11.00–18.00 Tues–Sun, closed Mon except Bank Holidays **ⓝ** Bus: 1, 9, 10, 22, 24, 29, 120, 126, 128

National Indoor Arena (NIA)

Where three canals meet you will find the National Indoor Arena. This venue has hosted International Athletics meetings, European Championship Gymnastics and other indoor sporting

events. It also hosts concerts, conferences and exhibitions.
🅐 King Edwards Road 🕿 0121 780 4141 🆆 www.thenia.co.uk
🅔 info@negroup.co.uk 🅝 Bus: 1, 9, 10, 22, 24, 29, 120, 126, 128

Royal Birmingham Society of Artists (RBSA)

One of the oldest art societies in Britain, the RBSA has two
galleries that show a changing exhibition of members',
associates' and friends' works. It also occasionally has visiting
exhibitions. 🅐 4 Brook Street 🕿 0121 236 4353 🆆 www.rbsa.org.uk
🅔 secretary@rbsa.org.uk 🕓 10.30–17.30 Mon–Fri, 10.30–17.00 Sat,
13.00–17.00 Sun 🅝 Tram: St Paul's; Bus: 101

St Paul's Gallery

Housed in this vast warehouse-style building is the largest
contemporary art collection outside London. The gallery
contains one of the most comprehensive collections of signed
album artwork from the likes of The Who, Eric Clapton, Pink
Floyd and Led Zeppelin. 🅐 94–108 Northwood Street
🕿 0121 236 5800 🆆 www.stpaulsgallery.com
🅔 info@stpaulsgallery.com 🕓 10.00–18.00 Mon–Sat, 11.00–15.00
Sun 🅝 Tram: St Paul's; Bus: 101

RETAIL THERAPY

The Mailbox Once Birmingham's main sorting office, The
Mailbox has been converted into a chic upmarket shopping
complex. Designer stores like Harvey Nichols, Armani and Hugo
Boss fill the once cavernous interior of the utilitarian building.
There is a wide range of eating and drinking places, many of

which overlook the canal basin at the back. The Mailbox is also home to **BBC Midlands** and its production studios. The long-running Radio 4 soap opera, *The Archers*, is produced here. Part of the complex is also the **Malmaison Hotel**. To the rear of the building is **The Cube**, a 17-storey contemporary designed complex with a rooftop restaurant and its own complex of canalside shops, apartments, hotel and café-bars.
ⓐ Wharfside Street ① 0121 632 1000 ⓦ www.mailboxlife.com
ⓔ info@mailboxlife.com ⓛ 24 hours daily; check with individual shops for their opening hours ⓝ Bus: 20, 61, 62, 63, 80, 87

TAKING A BREAK

Strada £ ❼ Strada serves contemporary Italian food ideal for lunch or dinner. Good views of the canal. ⓐ 8 Quayside
① 0121 212 2661 ⓦ www.strada.co.uk ⓝ Bus: 1, 9, 10, 22, 24, 29, 120, 126, 128

Away2Dine ££ ❽ Cruise the canals while eating food freshly cooked on board the boat. Large panoramic windows and floodlights provide ever-changing views of the canalside in both summer and winter. ⓐ 3 Brindleyplace ① 0845 644 5244
ⓦ www.away2dine.co.uk ⓔ enquiries@away2dine.co.uk
ⓝ Bus: 1, 9, 10, 22, 24, 29, 120, 126, 128

Café Ikon ££ ❾ A menu of Spanish tapas, delicious desserts and, on Wednesday evening, live flamenco and gypsy jazz guitar music. ⓐ 1 Oozells Square, Brindleyplace ① 0121 248 3226
ⓦ www.ikon-gallery.co.uk ⓝ Bus: 1, 9, 10, 22, 24, 29, 120, 126, 128

Handmade Burger ££ ⑩ Does what it says on the sign. This eatery serves up handmade creative burgers in a stylish setting right beside the canal. Ideally placed for a pre- or post-performance meal at the Symphony Hall. ⓐ The Water's Edge, Brindleyplace ⓣ 0121 665 6542 ⓦ www.handmadeburger.co.uk ⓝ Bus: 1, 9, 10, 22, 24, 29, 120, 126, 128

AFTER DARK

Bars & restaurants

Bar Risa/Jongleurs ⑪ A huge venue with comedy shows every Thursday, Friday and Saturday night. After the comedy there is dancing upstairs to classic hits of the 1960s, 70s and 80s. ⓐ Quayside Tower, Broad Street ⓣ 0870 787 0707 ⓦ www.risa-birmingham.co.uk ⓔ barrisa.birmingham@regent-inns.plc.uk ⓝ Bus: 1, 9, 10, 22, 24, 29, 120, 126, 128

The Jam House ££ ⑫ Jools Holland is the music director of this live music venue that serves up a varied menu of live jazz acts. There's also a very good restaurant and bar. ⓐ 3–5 St Paul's Square ⓣ 0121 200 3030 ⓦ www.thejamhouse.com ⓔ info@thejamhouse.com ⓝ Train: Snow Hill; Tram: St Paul's; Bus: 101

The Oriental Restaurant £££ ⑬ This canalside restaurant brings together dishes from Malaysia, China and Thailand, all presented in the most exquisite manner by a Thai food carving expert. ⓐ The Mailbox ⓣ 0121 633 9988 ⓦ www.theoriental.uk.com ⓔ info@theoriental.uk.com ⓝ Bus: 20, 61, 62, 63, 80, 87

Pushkar £££ ⑭ Modern North Indian dining fused with a little Western European cuisine makes this restaurant unique. With stylish, chic surroundings and very attentive staff. ⓐ 245 Broad Street ⓣ 0121 643 7978 ⓦ www.pushkardining.com ⓔ info@pushkardining.com ⓝ Bus: 1, 9, 10, 22, 24, 29, 120, 126, 128

Theatre & concert hall

Repertory Theatre ⑮ Next to the ICC, 'The Rep', as it is known, has been around since the 1970s. It is well known for the high calibre of its productions, its innovative approach to theatre and for making theatre accessible to everyone. ⓐ Broad Street/Centenary Square ⓣ Box office: 0121 236 4455 ⓦ www.birmingham-rep.co.uk ⓔ stage.door@birmingham-rep.co.uk ⓝ Bus: 1, 9, 10, 22, 24, 29, 120, 126, 128 ⓘ Admission charge

Symphony Hall ⑯ Constructed over a mainline railway tunnel, to eliminate the sound of trains the building rests on giant rubber bearings. When the hall is filled with over 2,000 people at a concert, it sinks several centimetres. The hall's acoustics are considered to be among the best in the world, as the huge baffles can be moved to tune the auditorium like some giant instrument. ⓐ Broad Street/Centenary Square ⓣ Box office: 0121 780 333 ⓦ www.thsh.co.uk ⓔ Box office: boxoffice@thsh.co.uk ⓝ Bus: 1, 9, 10, 22, 24, 29, 120, 126, 128 ⓘ Admission charge

Outside the centre

Birmingham was originally one of a number of small villages in an extensive forest – the reason why there are still so many green spaces and trees in the city. What are now the suburbs were themselves self-contained villages. Suburban transport and the development of manufacturing saw these villages expand. Birmingham's expansion was rapid and these villages were quickly absorbed into the greater conurbation. With the notable exception of Edgbaston, where the landowners refused to allow factories to be built, industry moved out from the centre to the surrounding countryside. Today, there are only reminders that the suburbs were indeed leafy villages with their own distinct community life in the form of mills, inns and taverns, churches and manor houses.

SIGHTS & ATTRACTIONS

Aston Hall

Recently opened after a £13 million refurbishment, Aston Hall is one of the finest examples of a Jacobean mansion in Britain, set in 21 hectares (52 acres) of parkland. Ceilings, wood panelling, fireplaces and friezes are among some of the outstanding features of this magnificent house, which also contains a cantilevered wooden staircase. It has received royalty on more than one occasion, most notably King Charles I prior to the Battle of Edgehill in 1642. The Astonish Gallery takes visitors on a journey through the history of the Aston area, including its sporting achievements (the hall is close to Villa Park, home to

Birmingham's most successful football club, Aston Villa).
ⓐ Trinity Road, Aston ⓣ 0121 675 4722 ⓦ www.bmag.org.uk
ⓔ aston.hall@birmingham.gov.uk ⓛ 12.00–16.00 Tues–Sun,
closed Mon except Bank Holidays (Apr–Oct) ⓝ Train: Aston or
Witton; Bus: 7, 11, 65, 104, 105

Bell's Farm

This timber-framed building has been restored but little altered
since the 16th and 17th centuries. The focus here is on the
teaching of traditional crafts. ⓐ Bell's Close, Druid's Heath
ⓣ 0121 433 3532 ⓦ www.bellsfarm.org.uk ⓛ By appointment
ⓝ Bus: 50

Visit the magnificent Jacobean Aston Hall

Birmingham Botanical Gardens

Designed by John Claudius Loudon, pioneer of landscaping
public open spaces, these beautiful gardens cover 6 hectares
(15 acres). There are four glasshouses and several important
plant collections, including the National Bonsai Collection.
There's also a discovery garden for children, a collection
of exotic birds, a café and Sunday music on the bandstand.
🅐 Westbourne Road, Edgbaston 🅣 0121 454 1860
🅦 www.birminghambotanicalgardens.org.uk 🅛 09.00–19.00
Mon–Sat, 10.00–19.00 Sun (Apr–Sept); 09.00–17.00 or dusk if
earlier Mon–Sat, 10.00–17.00 or dusk if earlier Sun (Oct–Mar)
🅝 Train: Five Ways; Bus: 10, 22, 23, 24, 29 🅘 Admission charge

Blakesley Hall

This 400-year-old Tudor timber-framed house was built by
Richard Smalbroke, one of Birmingham's leading 16th-century
merchants. Some of the original furniture remains and there
is also a walled herb garden and orchard. 🅐 Blakesley Road,
Yardley 🅣 0121 464 2193 🅦 www.bmag.org.uk
🅔 blakesley.hall@birmingham.gov.uk 🅛 12.00–16.00 Tues–Sun,
closed Mon except Bank Holidays (Apr–Oct) 🅝 Train: Stetchford;
Bus: 11, 55, 94, 97, 97a

Bournville Village

When George Cadbury relocated his chocolate factory from
Bridge Street in central Birmingham to a more rural location, it
was for the benefit of his employees and would 'alleviate the evils
of modern more cramped living conditions'. It was to be a model
village with wide-open spaces, schools, playing fields and a library

well as less cramped housing for Cadbury's workers. Because Cadbury was a Quaker, the village had no public house, a rule that has remained in place to this day, though there is a licensed members' bar. Bournville is still home to the Cadbury factory and its dark chocolate is named Bournville after the village. ⓐ Visitor Centre, Village Green, Bournville ⓝ Train: Bournville

🔺 *The timber-framed exterior of Blakesley Hall*

Cadbury World

This museum and factory tour is at Cadbury's manufacturing base in Bournville. It is a self-guided tour that takes you through the process from cocoa farm to the finished product using video, animatronics, exhibitions and a route through the factory. Advertising Avenue takes you back through your childhood memories of years of advertising. There are, of course, some free samples of the Cadbury products along the way. ⓐ Bournville ⓣ 0845 450 3599 ⓦ www.cadburyworld.co.uk ⓒ Open daily Mar–Oct (times vary so check website for details); limited opening Nov–Feb (check website) ⓝ Train: Bournville; Bus: 45, 47 ❶ Admission charge

Cannon Hill Park

The park was a gift to the people of Birmingham from a wealthy landowner. There are landscaped gardens, playgrounds, boating lakes and a cycling route providing open-air recreation for the city dwellers of Birmingham from the 19th to the 21st centuries. Ducks, geese and swans were introduced to the park, and adjacent to the park is the **Birmingham Nature Reserve** with animals, many of them British, in enclosures that are laid out in a way that is as similar to their natural environment as possible. ⓐ Edgbaston Road, Edgbaston ⓦ www.birmingham.gov.uk/parks ⓒ 24 hours daily ⓝ Bus: 35, 45, 47

Perrott's Folly

A tall octagonal tower with battlements was built by John Perrott, some say to spy on his unfaithful wife, and used

variously as an observatory and weather station. Along with the nearby brick Victorian Tower of the Edgbaston waterworks, it provided the inspiration for J R R Tolkien's Minas Morgul and Minas Tirith, the 'Two Towers' of Gondor. Both are on the Tolkien Trail. ⓐ Waterworks Road, Edgbaston
ⓦ www.perrottsfolly.co.uk ⓝ Bus: 8A, 8C

Sarehole Mill

This working watermill is one of only two remaining of the seventy that once graced the rivers of Birmingham. The mill and mill pond have several historical connections. Matthew Boulton rented the mill before setting up his Soho Manufactory. It was also the childhood playground of J R R Tolkien and, along with the village of Sarehole, is likely to have been the inspiration of 'The Shire', home to the Hobbits. The mill pond is part of a nature reserve.ⓐ Cole Bank Road, Hall Green ⓣ 0121 777 6612
ⓦ www.bmag.org.uk ⓔ bmag_enquiries@birmingham.gov.uk
ⓛ 12.00–16.00 Tues–Sun, closed Mon except Bank Holidays (Apr–Oct) ⓝ Bus: 5, 11

Shakespeare Express

This mainline steam locomotive with vintage carriages has a regular service from Birmingham to Stratford-upon-Avon. The outward and return journeys take a different route, giving passengers a different experience on both legs of their journey, and are well timed to allow for a good amount of time sightseeing in Stratford. Dining on the train is also available.
ⓐ Office: Warwick Road, Tyseley; Trains depart Snow Hill and Moor Street Stations ⓣ 0121 708 4690

Ⓦ www.vintagetrains.co.uk Ⓔ office@vintagetrains.co.uk
Ⓛ Check website or telephone for timetable Ⓝ Train: New Street,
Snow Hill, Moor Street; Tram: Snow Hill; Bus: Any bus service to
city centre ❶ Fare payable

🔺 *There is a Hobbit connection to Sarehole Mill*

Soho House

It was in the dining room of this 18th-century house that the Lunar Society often met. The Lunar Society consisted of the leading industrialists and inventors of the Industrial Age and included men like Josiah Wedgwood, James Watt, Joseph Priestley and Matthew Boulton, whose house it was. ⓐ Soho Avenue, Handsworth ⓣ 0121 554 9122 ⓦ www.bmag.org.uk ⓔ soho.house@birmingham.gov.uk ⓛ 12.00–16.00 Tues–Sun, closed Mon except Bank Holidays (Apr–Oct) ⓝ Bus: 74, 78, 79

◐ *Reflecting brilliance: Soho House was the meeting place for the Lunar Society*

Sutton Park

A former royal deer park, Sutton Park is made up of a mosaic of ancient heathland, woods, wetlands and lakes. It is Britain's largest urban nature reserve: Exmoor ponies and cattle roam free and there is an abundance of bird, animal and plant life. The park also contains historic features such as burial mounds and a Roman road. There are a number of heritage trails in the park and plenty of paths for strolling or hiking. The Visitor Centre offers guided walks and information leaflets on different aspects of the park. ⓐ Sutton Coldfield ① 0121 355 6370 ⓦ www.birmingham.gov.uk/parks ⓛ 24 hours daily ⓝ Train: Sutton Coldfield; Bus: 6, 902, 904, 905 ① Free entry but pay and display parking

CULTURE

Barber Institute of Fine Arts

The building in which the Barber Institute of Fine Arts is housed was purpose built and is one of the finest Art Deco buildings in the country. Opened in 1939, its galleries contain works by Monet, Manet, Renoir, Rubens and Rodin as well as Van Gogh, Gainsborough, Turner, Gauguin and Picasso. There is also an impressive coin gallery and accompanying exhibition on the role that Birmingham and Matthew Boulton played in standardising coinage not just in Britain but worldwide. ⓐ University of Birmingham, Edgbaston ① 0121 414 7333 ⓦ www.barber.org.uk ⓔ info@barber.org.uk ⓛ 10.00–17.00 Mon–Sat, 12.00–17.00 Sun ⓝ Train: University; Bus: 61, 62, 63, 885, 886

TAKING A BREAK

Punjab Paradise £ Family run for many years, this restaurant in the Balti Triangle prides itself on its customer care and its unique balti dishes. ⓐ 377–379 Ladypool Road, Sparkhill ⓣ 0121 449 4110 ⓔ tnc75uk@yahoo.co.uk Ⓝ Bus: 2, 3, 5, 6, 8C, 37

Simpsons Restaurant £££ A Michelin-starred restaurant run by a trio of award-winning chefs serving light modern dishes based on classical French cuisine. ⓐ 20 Highfield Road, Edgbaston ⓣ 0121 454 3434 Ⓦ www.simpsonsrestaurant.co.uk ⓔ info@simpsonsrestaurant.co.uk Ⓝ Bus: 21, 22, 23, 24, 29

AFTER DARK

Entertainment complex
Star City This vast neon-lit entertainment venue houses one of Europe's biggest multiplex cinemas. Inside, you'll find a bowling alley, indoor golf complex, multi-gym, climbing wall, and brand new Laser Station, as well as a large selection of places to eat and drink. It's also the venue for family-oriented events and world-class acts such as Cirque du Soleil and the Chinese State Circus. ⓐ Off Lichfield Road, Nechells ⓣ 0121 327 1140 Ⓦ www.starcity.org.uk ⓔ reception@starcity.org.uk Ⓝ Train: Aston; Bus: 66, 66A

▶ *The medieval Dudley Castle*

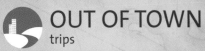
OUT OF TOWN
trips

Shakespeare Country

Birmingham promotes itself as the gateway to the heart of Britain, for which it is well placed. The two most popular areas to visit are Shakespeare Country to the southeast, and the Black Country to the northwest. **Shakespeare Country** includes Stratford-upon-Avon, Warwick and Warwick Castle. The **Black Country** (see page 84) includes places like Walsall and Dudley.

GETTING THERE

Easily accessible by train, services to Solihull, Warwick and Stratford-upon-Avon leave from Moor Street Station. A steam train service, the **Shakespeare Express**, departs from Snow Hill and Moor Street stations to Stratford-upon-Avon.

If driving, take the A34 to Stratford-upon-Avon and the A41, M42, M40 to Warwick. Stratford-upon-Avon is 40 km (25 miles) away and takes about 50 minutes to reach. Warwick is 37 km (23 miles) away and takes about 45 minutes to reach.

SIGHTS & ATTRACTIONS

Heritage Motor Centre, Gaydon
Appropriate for a city that was synonymous with the manufacture of some of Britain's most iconic cars, this museum houses a collection of vehicles that focuses on Britain's motoring heritage. ⓐ Banbury Road ❶ 01926 641 188 ⓦ www.heritage-motor-centre.co.uk ⓔ enquiries@heritage-motor-centre.co.uk ⓛ 10.00–17.00 daily ❶ Admission charge

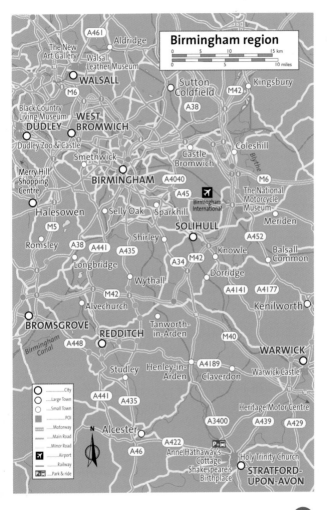

Birmingham region

0   5   10   15 km
0   5   10 miles

A461 Aldridge

The New Art Gallery
Walsall Leather Museum
WALSALL
M6
Sutton Coldfield
M42 Kingsbury
A38
Black Country Living Museum
WEST BROMWICH
DUDLEY
Dudley Zoo & Castle
Smethwick
Castle Bromwich
Coleshill
Blythe
Merry Hill Shopping Centre
BIRMINGHAM
A4040
M6
The National Motorcycle Museum
A45
Birmingham International
Halesowen
Selly Oak
Sparkhill
Meriden
M5
SOLIHULL
Romsley
A38 A441
Shirley
A435
Knowle
A452
Balsall Common
Longbridge
A34 M42
Dorridge
Wythall
A4141 A4177
M42
Alvechurch
Kenilworth
BROMSGROVE
REDDITCH
Tanworth-in-Arden
M40
Birmingham Canal
A448
WARWICK
Studley
Henley-in-Arden
A4189
Warwick Castle
A441 A435
Claverdon
Heritage Motor Centre
A3400
A439 A429
N
Alcester
A422
A46
Anne Hathaway's Cottage
Shakespeare's Birthplace
Holy Trinity Church
STRATFORD-UPON-AVON

○ ....City
◎ ....Large Town
○ ....Small Town
▪ ....POI
▬▬ ....Motorway
▬▬ ....Main Road
▬▬ ....Minor Road
✈ ....Airport
▬▬ ....Railway
P&R ......Park & ride

National Motorcycle Museum, Solihull

Completely destroyed by fire in 2003, this museum has risen
from the ashes despite losing many exhibits. The museum
charts the history of the motorcycle from its early beginnings
to the powerful machines of today. ⓐ Coventry Road, Bickenhall
ⓣ 01675 443 311 ⓦ www.nationalmotorcyclemuseum.co.uk
ⓛ 09.30–17.30 daily ⓘ Admission charge

Stratford-upon-Avon

Stratford-upon-Avon, southeast of Birmingham, has achieved
fame through the 16th-century playwright William Shakespeare,
who lived and was buried here.

Holy Trinity Church, the 13th-century church on the bank of
the River Avon, is the final resting place of the 'Bard' (William
Shakespeare). ⓐ Southern Lane ⓣ 01789 266 316
ⓦ www.stratford-upon-avon.org ⓛ 09.00–17.00 Mon–Sat, 12.30–
17.00 Sun (Mar & Oct); 08.30–18.00 Mon–Sat, 12.30–17.00 Sun
(Apr–Sept); 09.00–16.00 Mon–Sat, 12.30–17.00 Sun (Nov–Feb)

Owned and run by the Shakespeare Birthplace Trust, five
houses have some association with the playwright: Mary
Arden's Cottage, Nash's House and New Place, Hall's Croft, Anne
Hathaway's Cottage and Shakespeare's Birthplace.

Anne Hathaway's Cottage is a beautiful thatched cottage
with a typical English 'country cottage' garden and lies about
a mile from the centre of town. Anne, who was later to become
Shakespeare's wife, lived here as a girl and there are many rare
family heirlooms on display in the authentically restored rooms.
Tours of the garden are available in the summer months.
ⓐ Cottage Lane, Shottery ⓣ 01789 292 100

ⓦ www.shakespeare.org.uk ⓛ 09.00–17.00 daily (Apr–Oct)
❶ Admission charge

Shakespeare's Birthplace, in the centre of Stratford, is probably where the playwright was born, and he certainly spent much of his early married life here. The house has been a visitor attraction for over 250 years, and you can follow in the footsteps of prominent writers such as Charles Dickens and Thomas Hardy by signing the visitor's book. ❸ Henley Street

🔺 *Anne Hathaway's Cottage, historic and picturesque*

☎ 01789 204 016 **⊛** www.shakespeare.org.uk **◷** 09.00–18.00 daily (July & Aug); 09.00–17.00 daily (Apr–June, Sept & Oct) **❶** Admission charge

Warwick Castle

This well-preserved medieval castle has state rooms, a chapel and great hall, as well as dungeons, a torture chamber, towers and ramparts. Live shows that include jousting, combat, archery and falconry make this an ideal family day out. The castle houses the world's largest trebuchet, or catapult, which is fired twice daily. **ⓐ** Warwick **☎** 0871 265 2000 **⊛** www.warwick-castle.co.uk **◷** 10.00–18.00 daily (Apr–Sept); 10.00–17.00 daily (Oct–Mar) **❶** Admission charge

TAKING A BREAK

Dirty Duck/Black Swan The pub with two names is popular among the thespian community as a place to hang out after shows. The wall panels of the Actors Bar are adorned with photographs of those who have wined and dined here. **ⓐ** Waterside, Stratford-upon-Avon **☎** 01789 297 312 **⊛** www.dirtyduck-pub-stratford-upon-avon.co.uk

Marlowe's Restaurant ££ An Elizabethan restaurant in the centre of Stratford with original beams and oak panelling. The great and good of English theatre have dined here; autographed photos of the likes of Sir Alec Guinness, Sir John Gielgud, Sir Ralph Richardson and Vanessa Redgrave adorn the walls of the bar. **ⓐ** 18 High Street **☎** 01789 204 999 **⊛** www.marlowes.biz

AFTER DARK

Theatre

Royal Shakespeare Theatre Home of the Royal Shakespeare Company, at the time of writing the £100 million redevelopment was still under way, but is due to be completed by the end of 2010. This is the place to go if you want to see Shakespeare's plays. ⓐ Waterside, Stratford-upon-Avon ⓣ 0844 800 1100 ⓦ www.rsc.org.uk

ACCOMMODATION

Mercure Shakespeare ££ This 74-bedroom hotel dates back to 1637. Each room is named after a character in one of Shakespeare's plays. ⓐ Chapel Street, Stratford-upon-Avon ⓣ 01789 294 997 ⓔ h6630-gm@accor.com

The Arden Hotel £££ Located opposite the Royal Shakespeare Theatre this hotel, like the theatre, has undergone major refurbishment. It has 45 bedrooms, a brand-new brasserie and alfresco dining. ⓐ Waterside, Stratford-upon-Avon ⓣ 01789 298 682 ⓦ www.theardenhotelstratford.com

The Black Country

The Black Country got its name from the smoke belching out of the ironwork foundries and the dark spoil from relatively shallow coal mines. It is made up of the Dudley, Sandwell, Wolverhampton and Walsall metropolitan areas.

GETTING THERE

From Birmingham New Street there are regular train services to Sandwell and Dudley. The Metro operates from Snow Hill Station to Wolverhampton.

By car, take the A41 from the city centre, then the M5 south to Junction 2 and finally the A4123 to Dudley. For Walsall, take the A38(M) and M6 to Junction 9. Bus service 126 will take you to Dudley and the X51 will take you to Walsall.

SIGHTS & ATTRACTIONS

Black Country Living Museum, Dudley

This open-air museum occupies 10.5 hectares (26 acres) of a former railway goods yard. Historic buildings have been moved and rebuilt on the site to give an insight into life in the Black Country in the 19th and 20th centuries. Volunteers in period costumes guide visitors around. Electric trams and trolley buses transport visitors to the re-created village area, complete with an early-20th-century street that has a pub, sweet shop and Methodist chapel. There's also a Victorian schoolroom.

In addition, visitors can enjoy the traditional fun fair and a trip on a narrowboat to explore the Dudley Tunnel, where the canal goes under the town. ⓐ Tipton Road ☎ 0121 520 8054 ⓦ www.bclm.co.uk ⏰ 10.00–17.00 daily (Mar–Oct); 10.00–16.00 Wed–Sun, closed Mon & Tues (Nov–Feb)

Dudley Zoo and Castle

There are 12 listed buildings in Dudley Zoo, most in the Art Deco style. The zoo has over 200 species, most of which are endangered and are the result of successful captive breeding programmes. The zoo is in the grounds of Dudley Castle, and entrance to the castle is included in the price of the ticket. The 11th-century medieval castle was partly demolished during the English Civil War and then destroyed by fire in 1750.
ⓐ 2 The Broadway ☎ 0844 474 2272 ⓦ www.dudleyzoo.org.uk ⓔ admin@dudleyzoo.org.uk ⏰ 10.00–16.00 daily (Easter–Sept); 10.00–15.00 daily (Oct–Easter) ⓘ Admission charge (includes entry to castle)

Walsall Leather Museum

Walsall was, and still is, the centre of the leather goods industry in England. Products ranging from equestrian gear made for the Royal Family to wallets for the 'man in the street' are all produced in Walsall. This museum gives an insight into the leather industry past and present, and is appropriately housed in an old leather factory. ⓐ Littleton Street West ☎ 01922 721 153 ⓦ www.walsall.gov.uk/leathermuseum ⓔ leathermuseum@ walsall.gov.uk ⏰ 10.00–17.00 Tues–Sat, closed Sun & Mon (Apr–Oct); 10.00–16.00 Tues–Sat, closed Sun & Mon (Nov–Mar)

CULTURE

New Art Gallery, Walsall

The New Art Gallery presents classic, modern and contemporary art in exciting, innovative and often challenging ways. There are works by Van Gogh, Monet, Picasso, Turner, Renoir and Constable. The £21 million building that houses the collections is a work of art in itself. ⓐ Gallery Square ❶ 01922 654 400 ⓦ www.thenewartgallerywalsall.org.uk ⓔ info@thenewart gallerywalsall.org.uk ⓛ 10.00–17.00 Mon–Sat, 11.00–16.00 Sun

RETAIL THERAPY

Merry Hill Shopping Centre Merry Hill is Britain's fourth-largest shopping centre measured on retail floor space. Situated beside the Dudley No 1 Canal, the centre is home to 350 retail outlets, an Odeon cinema and a marina area with several bars and restaurants. ⓐ Brierley Hill ❶ 01384 487 900 ⓦ http://uk.westfield.com/merryhill

TAKING A BREAK

The Crooked House Pub The pub where marbles seem to roll uphill before you have even had a single pint. Mining subsidence has caused the crookedness but it makes for a very characterful place for a drink or a bite to eat. ⓐ Coppice Mill, Himley, near Dudley ❶ 01384 238 583

◗ *Finding your feet in Birmingham is easy*